Christian Trézin

Curator of Chambord Castle

Wonderful Chambord

Translated by Angela Moyon

ÉDITIONS OUEST-FRANCE

13, rue du Breil, Rennes

Top : *A general view from the north-west.*

Middle : *The lantern tower.*

Bottom : *François I's bedchamber.*

Front cover : *The north wall of the keep.*

Back cover : *An aerial view.*

Chambord at dawn.

Preface

This book describes one of the largest castles in the country, an image of France that has acquired world-wide recognition. It has been written for the general public and, because of this, there has been no attempt to include any detailed discussion of the questions and problems posed by this building. Nor is the work intended as a guide book. It is based on the most undisputed historical data and provides a fairly wide-ranging description so that anybody with an interest in the castle can begin to grasp its general significance. The book provides the reasons why it has been described as "wonderful", and encourages visitors to dig deeper into its background. This seemed to us to be the best form of discovery, and we have sequenced our description in what seemed to us to be the most natural way.

THE CHAMBORD ESTATE

The National Chambord Estate has belonged to the State since 1930. It consists of three entities that History has rendered inseparable viz. the castle, which represents the centrepiece of the estate, a park stretching over an area of 5,433 hectares, and a village with a population of 214. This is a statement of fact, but it is often forgotten and it conceals characteristics that make Chambord a quite exceptional spot. How many people know, for example, that the village of Chambord is the only one in France in which

the land and all the buildings belong to the State? There is no private property here. The population and shopkeepers are all tenants of the State. And how many people realise that the surface area of the park is comparable to the area of the city of Paris, unbelievable though that may be at first glance [1].

It was classified as a National Hunting Reserve in 1947 and is used by the Presidents of France for hunting. Both castle and park have been listed as historic monuments since 1840 and, since 1983, have been included in UNESCO's World Heritage list. It is one of the most popular of all French castles, and is one of the stately homes that symbolise France for the rest of the world. Almost 900,000 visitors or spectators entered the castle in 1991 or watched the events that were held there. But several hundred thousand more simply came to enjoy the natural environment - the forest and the animals at liberty in the park.

The Estate is run by several different government departments viz. the Ministries of Culture, Agriculture, the Environment, and Public Buildings and Works, and by other national agencies including the *Caisse Nationale des Monuments Historiques et des Sites* (the French equivalent of the British "National Trust"), the Forestry Commission, and the Hunting Commission. Actions and services are coordinated by an Estate Manager working with two assistants, the Director of the National Hunting Reserve who is responsible for the forest and the protection of the natural environment, and the castle's Curator.

(1) The length of the ring road in Paris, the "périphérique", is approximately the same as the length of the wall surrounding the Chambord Estate, i.e. almost 21 miles.

A deer in the forest.

Foreword

No discussion of Chambord would be complete without a reminder of a historical reality that is sometimes forgotten and seems totally paradoxical i.e. Chambord was a mere royal hunting ground in the midst of a forest in the days before plans were mooted to build a lodge for the sovereign and his Court. What happened next? The planned hunting lodge turned into a fabulous palace. It is the background to this complete change that is explored in this book and recounted in simple terms understandable by anybody with a wish to find out more about this unique building.

For the managers of the Chambord Estate, the general public is the major factor in every decision. Although every effort is made to provide the best possible amenities and cater for the widest possible range of interests, it must not be to the detriment of a place that is susceptible to damage. Consideration is currently being given to different ways of presenting the history of the estate and the outstanding architecture of the palace and its apartments, in an attempt to bring it to life while providing greater amenities for visitors and more extensive, high-quality information so that they can discover the natural resources of the Estate i.e. its flora and fauna. In fact, we are now making every effort to explain the complex, secretive world of Chambord without peeling away every layer of its mystery - and this book is part of this scheme.

Louis Hubert
*Commissaire à l'Aménagement
du Domaine de Chambord*

Introduction

Chambord deviates from the most commonly-held view of the Loire Valley Castles and the features that make them so attractive to visitors. You only have to think of the floral elegance of Azay-le-Rideau, Chenonceau or Talcy, the intimate luxury of Blois, the quiet strength of Chaumont, or the more austere charm of Ménars, Beauregard or Cheverny. And there are so many others, some famous, others less well-known, which could be taken as examples of the sweetness of life in the Loire Valley where the mild climate, infinite stretches of sky, memories of royal visitors and reminders of the Renaissance have accustomed people to an image of life here as pleasant and carefree.

Chambord has something quite different to offer visitors, a sight that is both powerful and dramatic. Everything about it is awesomely large. Indeed, it was considered as a gigantic building in its day. The village, prudently nestling some distance away, looks amazingly modest compared to this superb palace in which the stone changes colour depending on the time of day and the season of the year. It strikes the eye immediately, in a vast clearing that was cut from the heart of a forest encircled by 21 miles of walls, forming the largest walled estate in Europe. It is obvious that nothing about Chambord bears any relation to a country seat full of charm and gentleness. Yet by its very disproportion, its extraordinariness, and the particular aura of a castle that is described as virile when so many others try their female wiles on us [2], this residence is neither the result of mere chance nor the outcome of ordinary folly. It was a dream come true for a great king with a wish to amaze and impress Europe in a struggle for preeminence that brought him into conflict with Henry VIII of England and, more particularly, with Charles V, Holy Roman Emperor and King of Spain. The building commissioned by François I for Chambord had the same sort of panache as his campaign to capture the Duchy of Milan whic began with the Battle of Marignano, shortly after his accession to the throne. It was to be the finest of all castles for the man who had just become king at the dawn of a new civilisation, the Renaissance, a civilisation which gave mankind a new vision and an unsuspected power over the world in which he lived.

_____

[2] No woman has ever played an important role in the history of Chambord.

Overleaf : *Arriving at Chambord by the main courtyard.*

The village of Chambord.

La Thibaudière Lake.

THE CHAMBORD ESTATE [2 b]

The Chambord Estate lies on the edge of the Sologne area, only three miles from the R. Loire. A slow-flowing waterway, the R. Cosson, flows through it on its way to join the larger river. It was the existence of a "ford on the curve" of the Cosson which gave its name to the original hamlet ("camboritos" in Celtic parlance). It was a crossing point on a very ancient route through the marshlands in which the castle was built.

The limestone of the Beauce region can still be seen on the northern edges of the estate but the remainder is well and truly in Sologne, with sandy ground and a clay subsoil which makes this a land of water and forests with little in the way of agriculture. The lakes that give the area its own particular character also exist in the Chambord Estate, even if they are difficult to spot. The most striking feature of the estate is the magnificent forest, seen at its best in autumn when the leaves are changing colour. It is then that you can really appreciate the variety and balance of the different species of trees.

Stags, deer and wild boar roam at will here, as visitors are warned when passing through the gates - the Saint Dyé Gate if you arrive from the Loire. To the north and east are the Muides and Thoury Gates. If you cross the Boulogne Forest to the south, you will arrive at the Bracieux Gate. On the western side of the estate is the Chaussée-le-Comte Gate. Whatever your route, however, you cannot but be struck by the magical atmosphere that overwhelms you as you apparently step into another world, a place that seems to be cut off from the world outside by its wall, enclosing a unique universe forming a strange link between the wildlife and a unimaginable palace, a universe that suddenly comes into sight after a drive of only a few miles of road through the tall forest.

2 b. The information about the management of the forest and wildlife was provided by Mr. Francis Forget, Director of the Chambord National Munting Reserve, whom I should like to thank for his assistance.

The forest in the morning.

The existence of a well-stocked forest offering "deer.... in very great abundance", according to a historian named D'Avity, was the original reason for the building of a castle here. At least, to be more precise, it was François I's determination to acquire a estate on which he could satisfy his passion for hunting that resulted in the building of Chambord. He annexed part of the Boulogne Forest, which lay within the Crown-owned County of Blois, and purchased a few additional pieces of land to the north of the R. Cosson. Then, from 1542 onwards, he had the entire estate walled, so that the game could not stray outside. The length of the wall, after the estate had been extended towards Thoury at the request of Gaston of Orleans in 1645, exceeded 7 leagues, i.e. 21 miles. There were three gates in the wall at that time. By the 19th century, there were six. In addition to the five gates that still exist today, there was the Montfrault Gate to the south. The estate covered an area of 5,433 hectares and must have seemed vast, especially as it still is the most extensive estate in Europe.

It was large game that brought François I to Chambord, but he may have also been drawn to the place out of love. His mother, Louise of Savoie, Duchess of Angoulême, owned the estate and castle of Romorantin in Sologne. And it

A stag and wild boar.

The estate wall.

is said that François of Angoulême, the future King François I, loved the beautiful Countess of Thoury whom he met when he stayed in Romorantin and came to hunt in Chambord Forest with the sovereign, Louis XII. It is thought that these two passions led him to commission the building of a palace in this isolated forest. But it should be remembered that the royal castle of Blois is not far away

and that it was Blois which became François I's official residence and that of the Queen, Claude of France, Louis XII's daughter, who had lived in it all her life.

The history of this area, though, did not begin in the 16th century. A succession of domains and religious communities existed here in the Middle Ages. There are even the remains of feudal mottes, the earth mounds built in the 9th and 10th centuries and originally topped by castles. At that time, the area belonged to the Counts of Blois, of the House of Champagne. One of them, Thibaut the Cheat, was condemned for his maliciousness to spend his time in the next world leading a fearsome hunt through Chambord Forest. Sometimes, on autumn nights, a dark horseman can be seen galloping through the trees while, in the distance, can be heard the sound of a hunting horn and the barks of the hounds. But you will not be able to see and hear such sights unless you have first trodden the "grass that renders insane" and acts as an initiation rite in the Sologne of witches and warlocks.

In the 12th century, the mendicant Order of St. Etienne de Grandmont founded the Priory of Notre-Dame of Boulogne, and the canons of the Abbey of Bourg-Moyen in

A stag.

Blois founded the priory of Notre-Dame of Chambord. The Counts of Blois also owned a manorhouse in Montfrault [3] which was destroyed after 1785, and a castle in Chambord, a hunting lodge around which a small village soon developed. The history of this castle ended when François I decided to have it demolished and replaced by the castle we see today.

The idea of managing the estate's forest and natural breeding grounds grew up in the 19th century, after a national fund-raising scheme had made it possible to give the estate to the last member of the elder branch of the Bourbon family, in 1821. This was Henri of Bordeaux, the son of the assassinated Duke de Berry and the grandson of Charles X. More than one-half of the grounds were then worked by 23 farms or were given over to moorland or scrub, whereas in the previous century the estate had boasted 41 farms. The remainder of the land consisted of a deciduous forest. It was decided to replant the forest with a variety of different trees. In particular, 1,000 hectares were planted with Norway pines, a species that was previously unknown in the region but which was to spread over a wide area until it became typical of the landscape in So-

One of the estate entrances.

logne. The entire infrastructure as we see it today was built at that time i.e. the network of roads and avenues, the six gates, the area of forest, the network of drainage and the sewage system. Hunting was better organised and breeding

----

(3) To the south-east of the estate.

A forest path.

The "New" Lake.

of small game began towards the end of the century. People rode to hounds, in prestigious hunts that attracted packs such as those from Cheverny or belonging to General de la Rochejaquelin.

In 1930, the State became the owner of the estate as a whole and the Estates Office (*Service des Domaines*) was given overall responsibility for its running. Then, in 1947, the Chambord Estate was listed as a national hunting reserve and thereafter, it was the Water and Forest Department, followed by the Forestry Commission and National Hunting Department which took charge of its destiny. Now-adays, there are only two working farms. and, over the past 20 years, efforts have been made to create a new balance between the deciduous forest and the conifers which were planted in huge numbers throughout last century and up until 1954. These days, most of the young trees planted are oaks.

Yet the trees in the forest remain varied. Thickets of oaks, maritime pine or Corsican pines are the commonest, with their groves of young oaks and hornbeams. Between them are heaths or gorse-covered moors. There are also chestnuts, birches, alders, willows, robinias, blackthorn, hawthorns, and other berry-bearing trees.

The objective assigned to the Chambord Estate is to guarantee the perennity of the forest vegetation so that it provides cover and food for the wildlife. Some of the food is to be found on the browsing grounds [4] and, when need arises, more is available on the feeding grounds [5]. Timber production is of secondary importance. The wall round the estate ensures that large mammals breed here in large numbers, the commonest of all being stags and wild boars. But deer, moufflons, foxes, badgers, hares, rabbits, martens, and squirrels can also be seen. Numerous birds take advantage of this haven of peace and the special environments that continue to develop on the banks of the R. Cosson or the shores of the lakes, as is only to be expected in Sologne. Among the birds to be seen here are mallards, teal, herons, buzzards, snipe, pheasants, woodpeckers etc.

A large number of species are monitored on a permanent basis with a view to obtaining greater knowledge of their development. Many of them are protected species and, in Chambord, they find the tranquillity they need for breeding and development. The environment is particularly

---

(4) Well-tended meadows where game can find food.
(5) Areas in the forest to which cereals are brought.

The Cosson crossing.

suitable for the scientific study of deer and the Gabillière Farm to the north of the estate includes a documentation centre on this subject.

Species that cannot stray beyond the perimeter wall are checked for the purposes of annual removal, to ensure that excessive numbers do not upset the balance and perennity of the forest and, by extension, of their own future. Stags, for example, are taken alive [6] and sent either to restock forests in which the species has otherwise died out, or to strengthen existing populations or colonise new territory. Selective shooting is used to kill animals that are too old or too numerous. As to the rapid proliferation of wild boar, it is overcome by official hunts. It is in this highly-controlled framework that the presidential hunts are held, and Chambord is the most prestigious of them all. However, nobody has ridden to hounds here since the last war.

In order to ensure that this knowledge and outstanding environment are not reserved for specialists and technicians, numerous special events are held for school parties or adults to increase public awareness of nature in Chambord. Such events include courses, lectures, photography sessions, and wildlife filming sessions. To the general public, Chambord represents more than one thousand hectares laid out for their enjoyment and available at all times. Observation posts are accessible to all and, with patience and care, you may be fortunate enough to see and hear, alive and at liberty in their natural environment, the great mammals and all the other wildlife in one of Sologne' forests.

---

(6) In nets or panels, during operations known as panelling.

A public observatory on the edge of a wildlife watch area.

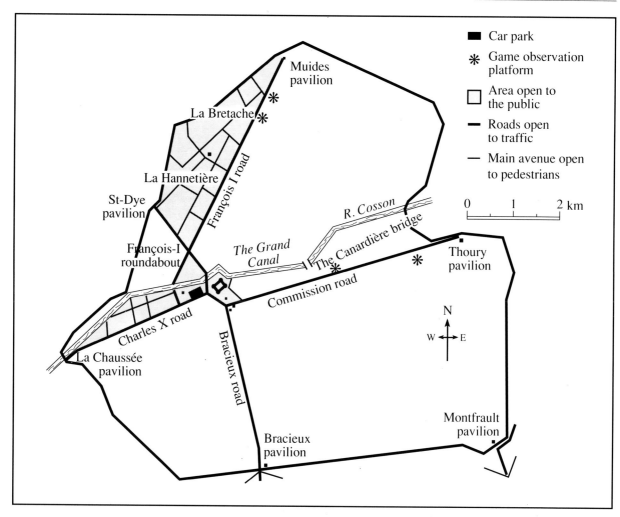

A plan of Chambord Estate.

CHAMBORD, AN EXPRESSION
OF THE ROYAL WILL

François I was passionately fond of hunting. When he mounted the throne, he was young, tall, strong, chivalrous, and handsome - and he loved women. He threw himself into the building of his palaces just as he threw himself, totally and unrestrainedly, into the Italian campaign, which was as brilliant as it was hopeless. In fact, the war cost him his freedom and a period of shameful captivity in Spain.

Another of his passions however, architecture, in which he apparently excelled, brought him enormous satisfaction. His castle in Chambord won him the admiration of Charles V, Holy Roman Emperor, his lifelong enemy, and the esteem of the whole of Europe. He had begun by having a decidedly Italianate wing added to the castle in Blois (1516-1518). He then went on to Chambord, launching in

1519 a project that would be finished by those who came after him. And, at the same time, in 1527, he began alterations on Fontainebleau and commissioned the building of the Château de Madrid in the Bois de Boulogne. This chateau no longer exists, but it was originally a hunting lodge designed along the same lines as Chambord. Other castles of the same type that were built for François I but have since disappeared include La Muette and Challuau. Villers-Cotterêts and Folembray were hunting lodges. Finally, he ordered alterations to the old royal castle of Saint-Germain-en-Laye, turning it into a grand residence, and, in 1546, commissioned Pierre Lescot to build the new Louvre Palace.

The young king's personality was marked by his passion for hunting and architecture, his love of women, and his taste for chivalry and derring-do, a taste that was slowly going out of fashion. All these facets of his character lay behind the will and determination that resulted in Chambord. In an estate well-stocked with game which he had himself created, a monarch like François I needed a hunting lodge, a castle big enough to accommodate his companions and their suites. But the building also had to be a source of amazement, something unique, a hunting lodge and meeting place for lovers' trysts. In fact, it became an incomparable palace, the largest one of its kind in those days. Standing alone deep in the heart of the forest!

It may even be compared to the fairytale palace of Apollidon the Magician, one of the characters in the Spanish prose romance of chivalry entitled "*Amadis de Gaul*" [7]. François I had first read the book during his captivity in Spain in 1525, and later had it translated. It proved to be a huge success. The entire Court read it, just as it had read the Ariosto's epic tale of "*Orlando furioso*" [8] in which adventure, love and marvels were recounted along with acts of heroism. There were also successful reprints of the "*Romance of the Rose*" [9] and the "*Quatre fils Aymon*" [10]. Bayard, the "knight who knew neither fear nor reproach" was the archetypal nobleman whose attitude remained indisputably mediaeval and who won himself the nickname "*furia francese*" during the Battle of Fornua. Admiral de Bonnivet, who led the Army at Pavia, even went so far as to declare that "[the French] are not accustomed to make war using military artifice. Instead, they fight with fine pennants unfurled". (An attitude which had a singular lack of success, it has to be said).

Yet this period of history, despite being steeped in images of a time long gone, had nevertheless discovered the upsurge and intellectual profusion of a modernity that

(7) It dated originally from the 14th century but was rewritten and altered by Montalvo between 1492 and 1502 and published in 1508.
(8) The work was published in 1516.
(9) A two-part poem written in the 13th century and updated into the French of the day by Clément Marot. It was reprinted fourteen times during the 16th century.
(10) A novel based on the gestual song entitled "*Renaud de Montauban*" dating from the 12th century. It was updated into the French of the day and reprinted twenty-five times in the 16th century.

Overleaf : *A view from the south-east.*

Riders in the forest.

A carriage ride.

latio studii", the return of ancient libraries to the Western World. People then rediscovered the philosophy and knowledge of the Ancients and, through them, the pagan humanism that believed in man's ability to understand the universe, hold it in his grasp and control it, independently of belief in God. In its wake came the joyous idea of the Golden Age, which became apparent again in the luxury and pleasures displayed by the Court, thanks to the return of peace and prosperity. Chambord belongs to this period of our history. The days of Ancient Rome and Greece, which Italy was the first to revive and which it then passed on in its own form of understanding, was a source of reverie for architects and men of letters alike.

rejected mediaeval values and it was living it to the full. The Renaissance, as it was to be called at a much later date, gained its most powerful expression in France through King François I. The world took on previously unsuspected dimensions. New continents were discovered; people began to use new techniques such as printing and navigational aids. Roman Catholicism had to withstand the onslaught of the Lutheran Reformation. Europe's new geopolitics, having been overturned by the fall of the Christian Empire in the Orient to the Turks [11] resulted in the "*trans-*

CHAMBORD - AN ITALIAN CASTLE OR A FRENCH CHATEAU?

After 1495, Charles VIII, having returned from his expedition to Naples [12] victorious but with no future ahead

---

(11) Constantinople was captured by the Turks in 1453.
(12) His aim was to recapture Naples which the Aragons had taken from the Angevins.

The castle seen from the south.

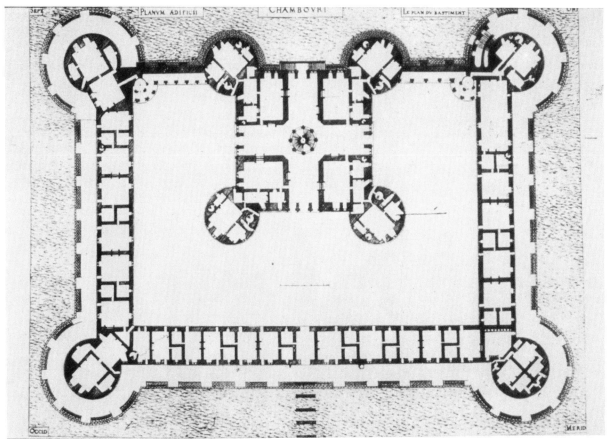

Designs for Chambord by Jacques Androuet du Cerceau.

of him, invited some twenty artists [13] to Amboise. Among them were engineers, landscape gardeners, and craftsmen. Commonly used in the commissions given by the King or others, the Italian forms of decoration, which had already made an appearance in Lyons and Provence, were to become more widespread, shaping the taste of clients in the Loire Valley before spreading similarly to the Paris Basin and to the whole of France.

Yet at the turn of the century, it would have been useless to seek, among these artists and craftsmen, architects bearing the title of architect and commissioned to carry out the type of work that we associate with this profession. It is true that, at that time in France, the idea had not yet acquired the meaning that was to be given to it over the following decades, the meaning that we know today. Domenico da Cortona, who built a number of wooden models corresponding to a variety of projects for castles including Chambord and was later responsible for the building of the Town Hall in Paris, was described as a "maker of castles and cabinetmaker". Curiously enough, Leonardo da Vinci, who is universally famous for his paintings and theoretical work, described himself first and foremost as an engineer, since, in his day, he had a reputation as a military engineer and an organiser of festivities. He was invited to France in 1516 by François I "to carry out work in architecture" and hydraulics. He arrived in 1517.

France was no longer unaware of what was happening in the Arts in Italy; it was an upsurge that could be seen in every nook and cranny of the wonders of Florence, Venice, and Rome. François I was even more aware of this than anybody else. Later, he was to further extend the Italian colony in France by inviting the painters and artists of every type who formed the Fontainebleau School. Work on Chambord, however, began in 1519. As there is no doubt that the castle bears the hallmark of Italy in its marvellous carvings, its arched galleries and its layout, it is among the Italian artists already in France at that time that we should seek the person, or persons, responsible for working on the

(13) Among the artists invited to France by Charles VIII were Domenico Bernabei, better-known as Domenico da Cortona or Le Boccador, "maker of castels and cabinetmaker".

The roof and top section of the castle.

project, designing it, or even acting as a source of inspiration for it.

Chambord, though, is also very French. Its layout is strangely reminiscent of Vincennes and other, less well-known, castles in which the keep has four towers and backs onto an enormous outer wall forming a quadrangle, with a tower at each corner. Towers have always been symbols of power. Is Chambord a mighty fortress within a plain, based on a well-known mediaeval design? It most obviously is not, despite the moat [13b], the apparent strength of the towers and the traditional military layout. Wars were no longer being fought on French soil when Chambord was built.

As to the roof bristling with tall chimneys, turrets, lantern turrets, huge ornate dormer windows and the vast central lantern tower, they are irresistible reminders of the *"Très Riches Heures du Duc de Berry"*, a set of miniatures dating from the end of the 14th century depicting the castles in Saumur and Mehun-sur-Yèvre, whose flamboyant outlines are comparable to those of Chambord in the profusion of architectural features forming a veritable forest at roof level. This is not just a fortuitous resemblance; it is an offshoot of earlier designs. The image of the heroic knight, whose daily existence brings him into contact with love and events of truly marvellous significance, is reflected here as it is in mediaeval literature. It should also be said in passing that it takes considerable technical prowess to build a 104-foot lantern tower at a height of 182 ft. above ground level. But out of all this, is it worthwhile looking for the designer, the architect indeed, from among the Frenchmen who acted as site overseers and who were, from the outset, known as "master stonemasons", rather than among the Italians? We shall try to come to a decision later.

---

13 b. In fact, the moat was commissioned by Louis XIV but was never completed.

The north wall.

CHAMBORD, A CASTLE STEEPED IN SYMBOLISM

If you want to really get to grips with Chambord, you have to take time to look at it closely. When you arrive from the north, you are faced with the great wall backing onto the flower beds. It is 169 yds. long and looks as if it is symmetrical, with its four towers, central doorway, and incredible pyramid of roofs culminating at the top of the great lantern tower. But if you look more closely, you will see that there are not the same number of windows to left and right, to East and West, and that there is a spur-shaped addition at the corner of the East Tower containing a staircase and François I's study on the first floor. In fact, this tower was built at a later stage in the construction to house the monarch's apartments and is linked to the inner tower by a wing topped by galleries. Originally, the king was to be accommodated in the tower to the left of the central doorway, but the size of the apartments was considered unworthy of such an august guest.

Although it was originally intended to build only the central section of the castle i.e. the keep topped by the two central towers, the change of plans placing the royal apartments to the East brought with it a need to design another symmetrical gallery wing, and to install the chapel in the opposite, West, tower. This being so, the frontage is flanked by the royal apartments and the chapel - God and the King symbolically shared power.

As you proceed to the West side of the castle, you will see a three-storeyed wing beyond the chapel tower as if continuing the great Northern wall. The same construction exists on the East side and both are linked to low wings roofed with terraces. There are towers at the corners. Another low wing closes off the South wall containing the "royal entrance", which opens opposite the keep. In all the castle forms a quadrangle measuring 169 yds. by 127 yds.

The chapel tower and wing.

Opposite : The Royal Entrance in winter.

Is it feasible to believe that the need for a hunting lodge was the sole reason for the building of Chambord? This may have been its main function but its design has other, quite different, meanings. Intellectually, politically and architecturally speaking, it was an outstanding project which has seldom been equalled, and the cost involved was stupendous, not to mention the cost of the constant restoration work required since the outset.

For many years, Chambord was only used for short periods at a time, hunting seasons ranging from a few days to a few weeks at the most. It was visited only by monarchs who were not put off by the difficulties involved in travelling with their suite and furniture and who were strongly motivated by the attractiveness of the superb setting. Yet even they were infrequent visitors. François I himself spent hardly more than three months here in all. Because of this, no real kitchens were built in the 16th century, despite the luxury of the palace as a whole, and the use of latrines on the ground floor or in the attics shows that there was no real intention to settle here permanently. Not until the 18th century was it lived in for a more or less

continuous period of some ten years and fitted out in consequence. Then, after 1789, it again suffered a long period of solitude, becoming the empty castle that it has constantly been ever since. What a strange destiny! It is perhaps understandable in a hunting lodge but is difficult to accept for such a superb building as this.

Riding to hounds, a reminder of François I's reign.

Chambord, as it stands, was the result of a great idea. It was intended as a symbol, an image in stone of the power of a king who was in the throes of developping the notion of the absolute monarchy, temporal authority set, as we have seen in the symmetry of the towers containing François I's apartments and the chapel, in opposition to the power of God from whom the sovereign acquired his legitimacy. This authority, though, is not shown as military might, in a massively overpowering castle. It is underlined by features designed to arouse a sense of wonderment in the monarch's subjects and in the world as a whole, by projects that are unique, projects like the literary outline of a literary castle. Every single feature of the building was designed with this aim in mind, its size, its references to traditional systems of defence, the startling modernity of the Italianate elements, the quality of the carvings, the amazing design of the roof, and the gold leaf used on the upper sections. And, to judge by contemporary reports, François I achieved his objective. Even Charles V, who remained his enemy throughout his reign, described it in 1539 as "an abbreviation of all that human industry can produce". Brantôme stated that "it could be counted among the miracles of the world". The great architect, Jacques Androuet du Cerceau, wrote in 1576 that "the entire building is admirable and a wondrously superb sight". In 1577, the Ambassador of Venice, Jérôme Lippomano, who was not known for his liking of France, declaimed ecstatically, "I have, in my life, seen several magnificent constructions, but none more beautiful and more ornate". And later, in the 17th century, André du Chesne confirmed that "Chambord is the most marvellous building in every respect compared to others in Europe".

CHAMBORD AND ITALY

Following the main current of inspiration for the artistic revival in France known as the Renaissance, Chambord borrowed from Italy an architectural idea that was among the most modern of its day and that was previously unknown in France, viz. a layout centred on the keep. All the rooms and apartments are built around the famous double-spiral staircase which extends into the great lantern tower

The plans of the keep.

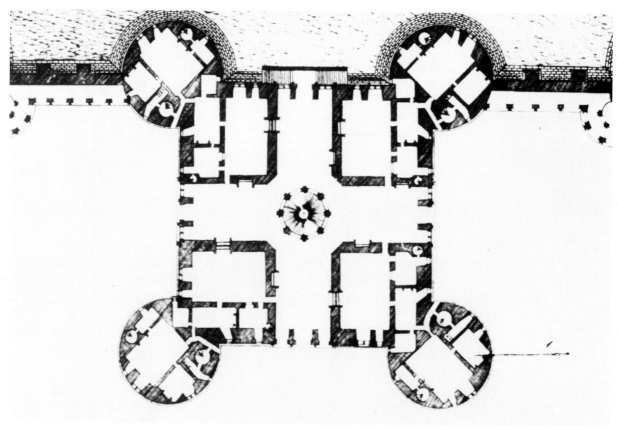

in the roof. The staircase was a feat of technical prowess in its day since it enabled two people, each climbing one of the two flights simultaneously, to see the other person without ever meeting him. Around the staircase on each floor are four identical rooms laid out in the form of a Greek Cross. The arms of the Cross divide the area into four quarters, each containing an identical independent apartment reached by the rooms within the Cross which serve as passageways. The same principle is applied throughout, from ground floor to roof terrace.

The towers at the corners also contain an independent apartment, each of them identical on each floor except for a few minor details. They are reached by external arched galleries running along the façade, linking them to the rooms within the Greek Cross. At terrace level, each tower has a pepperpot roof, while each quarter is topped by a square pavilion with a high roof. There is one apartment on the bottom floor and two attic floors above.

All the sections of the building are systematically laid out around the central feature of the design. Until then, nowhere in France had such attention been paid to a master plan, or abstract design, which was methodically imposed upon the construction in such a way that it determined the layout of the rooms in a castle and the way of life enjoyed therein.

It is indeed a concept which is obvious in the architecture here. Based on a return to the culture of Ancient Greece or Rome, the revival of Platonic ideas such as universal harmony and the possible attainment of essential truths through ideal, mathematical forms, led Italian architects and theoreticians to work on perfect, symmetrical, centred forms. The most significant of these were circles, Greek Crosses and spheres. The great lantern tower above the staircase can be considered, in Chambord, as a dome in a church, standing as it does at the centre of the Cross and providing the highest point in the building.

In its day, this centred layout could only be compared to the design of a few Italian churches, the most famous of which was Bramante's design for St. Peter's in Rome, dating from 1505. But Leonardo da Vinci also gave careful consideration to these questions and he drew a large number of projects for churches, and residences which were never built. For the apartments, a "common layout" was sometimes to be seen in the villas of Tuscany.

The plans showing their regular grid pattern.

The Dieudonné, Count of Chambord, Tower

The François I Tower

The Chapel Tower

The Robert of Parma Tower

The Dauphine wing

The François I wing

The Bell, or Henri IV Tower

The Caroline de Berry Tower

The Orleans Outhouses

The Princes' Tower

The Cauldron Tower

The Royal Entrance

The rationalisation of Chambord's layout goes even further as regards elements "borrowed" from Italy. It makes more systematic use of a grid or frame with sides measuring 49 yds. within which the layout is inserted. This system was also used in Chenonceaux and Bury, a castle which no longer exists, but less systematically. The keep completely fills one of the squares, each side being divided into 5, giving 25 squares measuring 10 yds. along each side. These squares define the position and size of the staircase, the cross-shaped rooms and the apartments, in a generally symmetrical layout.

The confirmation of royal authority is obvious, as we have seen, in the equivalent, although opposing, position within the design of the towers containing the king's apartments and the chapel. And, as if to underline this feature and give it a third dimension, the central staircase provides a link between earth and heaven, extending in a superbly ideal fashion into the traceried lantern tower whose final fleur-de-lys symbolically dominates the entire building from a height of 182 ft. François I had an idea of the meaning of his power, an idea that tended towards absolute monarchy, and he expressed it in another way by the inclusion of his emblem, the salamander wearing, not an open royal crown, but a closed imperial crown. Given his bitter struggle with Charles V for the title of Holy Roman Emperor, a title which he was unable to obtain even before the building of this castle, the political meaning of Chambord seems to be quite clear.

There are many other Italianate features contributing to the beauty of the castle as a whole. All the carvings, whether or not they were created by Italian artists, were inspired by Italian forms. The upper sections of the roofs are incrusted with geometrical patterns laid out in slate, which imitate the marble panelling on Milanese buildings in the 15th century, such as the Carthusian monastery in Pavia. The chambers on the second floor and François I's study, his Italian-style "*studiolo*", have decorated box ceilings similar to those common in the days of Ancient Rome, and they were a great novelty in France. The terrace and galleries from which guests could watch the hunt and the balustrade running along the entire building are, despite the French-style upper sections, decidedly Italian.

The upper section of the keep with its slate motifs.

THE EARLY BEGINNINGS OF THE DESIGN

To whom, then, can we ascribe this overall design which combines Italian features that were thitherto unknown in France at that time with layouts that were firmly fixed in tradition?

Domenico da Cortona was among the men who worked on a variety of projects that were submitted to François I. The "maker of castles and cabinetmaker", who was resident in Blois from 1512 to 1531, built wooden models for a number of buildings, windmills, bridges and castles, including some which may have been designed for Chambord. One of them, made c. 1519 and which then disappeared from view for many years, was seen and noted by Félibien, a 17th-century architect and historiograph. According to the drawings that have been preserved, the model showed only the keep, and it had a terraced roof, without any upper elements. The walls were broken up by arcading which was quite different to the final result. The layout, however, is very similar to the castle we see today, with the exception of the main staircase which was straight and built into one arm of the Cross. This idea may have been just too Italian to be accepted without alteration.

Leonardo da Vinci had also drawn a similar design for a villa in the Milan area. The two artists had known each other since Leonardo came to live in Le Clos-Lucé in Amboise. In 1517, he had answered a request from the King for a design for a vast castle in Romorantin. It was totally unconnected with the Chambord project, and was never built.

Leonardo da Vinci was also interested in multiple staircases as is obvious from one of his own drawings showing a staircase with straight flights of steps and four spirals placed in the centre of a building. The architect, Palladio, described it in 1570 as the Chambord staircase and although this is patently untrue, it shows the extent to which Leonardo's studies of this theme are apparently connected to the castle. It is more than likely that he was to thank for the central position of the staircase and the use of more than one spiral. However, the double spiral which was finally selected for Chambord might be a French variation of his four-spiral project, since the double spiral was not unknown in France and the traceried staircase, a piece of ostentatious daring shown off to its full advantage in Blois, is part and parcel of French tradition.

The designs submitted by Domenico da Cortona as noted by Félibien.

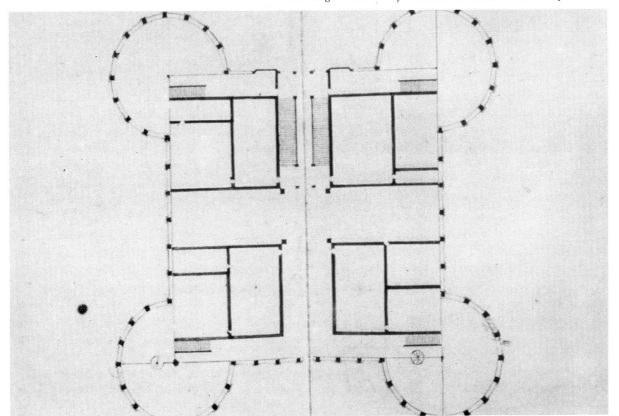

An aerial view.

Other essential features of the design can also be attributed to Leonardo da Vinci, such as the modular grid of the keep-centred layout, or the system of apartments and passageways. And there may be many more.

Despite the abundance of such contributions, it is difficult to imagine a single Italian architect who would, in 1515, have designed a castle with a keep, outer wall, and massive corner towers. Nor would an Italian have been likely to design the imaginative roofs and their upsurge of vertical elements or the façades that were marked off in grids by the set of double rows of horizontal moulding and pilasters that were interlinked from top to bottom. Not to mention the use of a vast, and singularly-obvious, traceried spiral staircase when, in Italian palaces, the staircases are straight and placed discreetly to one side.

If, for all these reasons, an Italian artist cannot have been the designer of the building as a whole (and it has to be said, as an aside, that such a state of affairs would not have escaped a mention in the chronicles of the day), who

can we point to? There are no known French architects in the first quarter of the 16th century. Even the great Jean Goujon was called "master-mason to the King". And it was this title of master-mason that began to feature in the archives with regard to those responsible for the royal building projects in Blois and, later, Chambord. They were Jacques, then Denis, Sourdeau, Pierre Nepveu known as Trinqueau, and Jacques Coqueau, all of them entrusted by the king with the building of his castles.

How should we understand this expression of trust? Was it based on the talent of those concerned and their capacity to produce buildings that were pleasing to the king? Or was it, as was common in those days, that the layout of the building was imposed by the person commissioning it, in this case the King who designed his ideal castle on the basis of the projects and suggestions submitted to him and who then entrusted the actual building work to master-masons, leaving them only very little scope for individuality in the work. Later in the century, the French architect Jacques Androuet Du Cerceau described François I's taste for creating buildings that he loved "marvellously" "so that it was the greatest of all pleasures for him". This would also explain, given the clumsiness of the builders, the large number of alterations or changes of mind which were made during the building, perhaps as a result of successive or contradictory decisions on the part of the royal personage.

In short, it is possible to imagine the stages that led to the general design of Chambord. Dominico da Cortona made one or more wooden models for the king, including a model of a castle which closely resembled an Italian design transposed onto a layout around a traditional French keep. Leonardo da Vinci then gave the project greater theoretical rigour by applying a modular grid pattern and placing a four-spiral staircase in the centre, while situating the apartments on a systematically regular layout. And finally the king, acting as architect, developed other projects with French master-masons who interpreted the Italian proposals and completed them in line with national conventions. The final choice was an architectural project that combined all the various suggestions. It was built by French master-masons.

THE MAIN STAGES IN THE BUILDING WORK

This building, which gives a real impression of overall unity, was not actually finished until c. 1690, some 170 years after construction work began in 1519. But the project and its main objective were still so strongly-maintained and so easily seen as a reflection of royal authority that even Louis XIV and Hardouin-Mansart, the architect who designed Versailles, believed it worthwhile to continue to build in accordance with the original designs, apart from a few, minor, details.

Although, on paper, the construction seemed to have last for a particularly long period, this should not be allowed to mask the truth. It did not really take all these years to build Chambord. Most of the work was completed in just 36 years. The initial work, which lasted from 1519 to 1535, saw the completion of the central part of the castle, the keep. Then, from 1535 to 1547, the outer walls were built, as were the lower wings up to the level of the first storey, the François I Wing to the east and the chapel wing to the west. After the death of King François I, his son, Henri II, added the second storey to the chapel wing, between 1547 and 1555, but did not complete the building and it remai-

Overleaf : *A close-up of the south wall of the keep.*

An aerial view of the keep.

François I's emblem, the salamander.

François I's cipher, a capital "F".

ned without rafters or roof until 1681. At that time, Louis XIV decided to commission Jules Hardouin-Mansart to complete this castle, while continuing the massive task of building Versailles.

The stone used in the building of Chambord is the same as that used in buildings throughout the Loire Valley. It is a soft limestone called "tuft". For Chambord, it was supplied by numerous quarries during the various stages in the building work i.e. Bourré, Lye, Apremont, Marnay, Cheillé, Foncher, and Saint-Cyr-en-Bourg. Not all the stone has withstood the test of time in the same way [14]. Most of it was brought to the site along the R. Loire and

[14] In more recent times, quarries in Villentrois have been supplying good-quality stone for restoration work.

Chambord as drawn by Jacques Androuet du Cerceai, with the lake on the north side in accordance with the original plans.

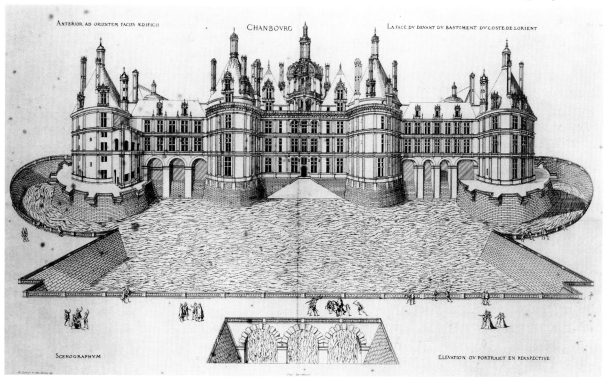

The François I Wing.

ably daring, the King had the idea of diverting one of the arms of the R. Loire so that it would flow past the new castle. In 1529, an Italian hydraulics engineer named Pietro Caccia da Novare was asked to submit a project but it was shelved because of the technical difficulties and astronomical costs involved. It was another Italian with more modest ideas, Paoul de Breignan, who diverted the course of the R. Cosson to comply with the wishes of the monarch. The layout of the waterways and fountains that was François I's dream, including a vast basin in front of the castle, is depicted in engravings made by Jacques Androuet Du Cerceau; it was not completed in François I's day. In the 17th and 18th centuries, major earthworks were dug in an attempt to bring the king's original intentions to life.

By 1539, everything seemed to have been finished in the keep, including the lead on the roof which was coated in gold leaf. It was during this year that Charles V was welcomed to the castle with a decor drawn from Ancient Greece. There were nymphs and representations of Diana the Huntress in the main chambers and apartments, in which frescoes, tapestries and ornate furniture had quickly been installed ready to receive him. The Spanish sovereign left Chambord amazed and astounded.

The South-East, or Henri V, Tower in the keep.

The chapel wing, completed during the reign of Louis XIV.

through the harbour set up in Saint-Dyé [15], a major river port which was also used for other supplies.

The initial building work began in 1519. At that time, the plan was to build a square castle to a centred layout, with four corner towers. Not until later was this construction given the name of "keep". It was particularly difficult to lay the foundations for such a massive building on marshland. A platform had to be built on oak piles sunk into the peat and it was consolidated several times, probably using rubble supplied by the demolition of the old castle. The work was subject to a number of mishaps, and the site closed down for two years, in 1525 and 1526, when François I was taken prisoner after the French defeat at Pavia and held captive in Spain. By that time, only the base of one tower was beginning to rise above ground level.

By the time the King returned, his ideas had matured. He had alterations made to the work and decided to add wings, at a later date, to the building that then became the "keep" of a much larger castle. The site work was re-organised and began again in earnest. But, as if to make things even more difficult or make the result even more admir-

(15) Three miles north of Chambord.

In 1535, work had begun on the outer wall and, in 1540, the first two storeys of the tower and wing containing the King's apartments were built at the eastern end, with the galleries linking them to the keep. But as yet this part of the building remained unroofed. The chapel tower, west wing and corresponding galleries were built to ground floor level. Work had started on the lower wings of the outhouses.

When François I died in 1547, the connecting galleries, the tower and the King's apartments were all completed. A spiral staircase known as "François I's stairs" had been added outside in the corner of the courtyard and there was an outer walkway across the top of a portico, linking it to the first floor of the keep. The chapel tower, west wing and galleries had reached first floor level. The chapel itself had progressed as far as its vaulted roof. Another outside staircase, this time traditionally known as "Henri II's stairs", was placed symmetrically opposite the one in the east courtyard. But the lower wings of the outhouses had still not been finished.

Henri II made a few additions to the building work, adding the second storey of the chapel wing, galleries and spiral staircase. But the building work was not completed in his reign and it remained open to the sky until the end of the 17th century.

Not until Gaston d'Orleans, Louis XIII's brother, took things in hand did the first major maintenance and restoration work take place, in 1641. Gaston d'Orleans lived in Blois and was finally exiled to the town.

Louis XIV took a great interest in Chambord. Between 1664 and 1685, he had the existing buildings refurbished and commissioned a number of alterations to the interior. He also ordered Hardouin-Mansart to complete the unfinished work i.e. the chapel, west wing and galleries, Henri II's stairs, and the lower wings of the outhouses onto which he commissioned the building of an upper attic storey that was decidedly lacking in good taste and has since been removed. It was also Louis XIV who commissioned the building of the "Royal Entrance" on the south side.

The architect's more ambitious plan, which involved completing the castle in accordance with 16th-century projects, was refused by the King. So great was his respect for the castle that he took care to ensure that his own new buildings had the "form, manner and decorative features such as those seen on the north tower and François I wing".

The Cosson Canal from the terrace.

Hardouin-Mansart therefore put most of his energy into transforming the castle's surroundings. The main aim of his project was to render the park healthier and more attractive by draining the marshland that had reformed as a result of the lack of upkeep, and diverting and canalising the R. Cosson. He also intended to dig a moat round the castle and lay out gardens including the great flower bed on the north side and the main courtyard to the south, flanked by vast stables. Only one stable block was ever built and then only partially; today, it lies in ruins.

The project was almost totally completed. Indeed, it was continued into the 18th century with the digging of the great canal on the eastern side.

CHAMBORD CASTLE AND ITS OCCUPANTS

Chambord was François I's first great architectural dream - and the most successful. He was extremely proud of it so much so, in fact, that he ordered the speeding up of the building work in order to be able to surprise Charles V with a visit to Chambord during the Spanish monarch's visit to France in 1539. "Let's go home," he used to say, when speaking of Chambord. He would probably have spent more time there if his determination to extend royal authority had not obliged him to reside rather longer in Paris, Fontainebleau, Saint-Germain-en-Laye or elsewhere in the Paris Basin than in the Loire Valley. He only came to Chambord to hunt. It is, though, difficult to imagine all that was involved when the King and his Court moved from one palace to another, complete with furniture, tapestries, valuables, clothes, weapons, plate and cooking utensils for several hundred people, from the noblest of lords down to the humblest of servants. It is said that thousands of horses were required when the Court travelled from Fontainebleau to Blois.

In fact, despite the stupendous cost of building this castle, it was used by the King for hunting perhaps once every two years - one hundred days in all over the remainder of his life. But the prey was both animal and human, and François I had had an apartment laid out near his own for his official mistress, Anne de Pisseleu, Duchess of Etampes. It is said that he was describing her when, using the diamond in his ring, he scratched on one of the windowpanes in his study, the famous saying,

Oft varies womankind
Naught but a fool believes her

of which there is a second version which runs

Oft varies womankind

A reconstruction of François I's bedchamber.

The coffered ceiling in the "studiolo".

*The bed in the François I Bedchamber decorated
with 16th-century Italian embroidery.*

François I's study, or "studiolo".

*Clumsy is he who believes her
or even a third which begins
All womankind varies*

It is also said that Louis XIV later smashed the windowpane bearing the saying, in order to please Mademoiselle de La Vallière. But other eye witnesses say that they read it in the recess of one of the windows in the royal

apartments, so who are we to believe? Let us leave the problem unsolved. François I never returned to Chambord after 1545.

Henri II continued the building work and also came here to hunt. In 1552, he signed a peace treaty here with German princes. Queen Catherine of Medicis, who was drawn to this spot for its magical atmosphere, is said to have climbed to the very top of the great lantern tower with her astrologers "in order to consult by night the sky and stars". Her sons, François II and Charles IX, both of them keen huntsmen, also spent a few, short periods here and tradition has it that the frail Charles IX even brought a stag to bay on the estate, alone and without his hounds.

The total lack of interest expressed in Chambord by Henri III and, more especially, by Henri IV plunged the castle into a deep sleep under the eye of its governors and captains of the royal hunt. Louis XIII was scarcely more enthusiastic about the castle and he enfeoffed his brother, Gaston of Orleans, with Chambord and the County of Blois. Gaston of Orleans settled in Blois Castle and became very attached to Chambord. Not only did he stay here frequently after 1641, but he was instrumental in ensuring its restoration from then until his death in 1660.

The chamber of the King's First Valet.

Thereafter Louis XIV, having realised the symbolism of a castle that represented absolute power, began to show an interest in Chambord. He was not content to commission Hardouin-Mansart to complete the original layout. Between 1660 and 1685, during his nine visits here, most of them lasting several weeks, he had alterations made to any features in the apartments which no longer corresponded to Court etiquette, the ceremonial and protocol which always accompanied any action on the part of the King. François I's apartments were considered to be too far removed from the centre of the castle and were abandoned. They were replaced by a totally new idea. Absolute monarchy demanded a quite different position for the sovereign and it seems to have been in Chambord that the idea of a row of royal apartments in the centre of the main façade of the castle was first tried. It was taken up again in Versailles. In order to make the alterations necessary for this change, the two north quarters on the first floor of the keep were completed and linked by the north chamber in the Greek Cross which then became an antechamber to the apartments. The continuous row of rooms enabled Court etiquette to instigate a hierarchy, or progression, in the granting of favours that brought people more or less close to the King, whose chamber was situated at the very end of the suite. The interior decoration included parquet flooring, wood panelling, and wall coverings consisting of silks and tapestries.

Festivities in Chambord were brilliant occasions, as was only to be expected, and they were attended by the same people as similar events in Versailles. Molière and Lulli wrote opera-ballets there, and "*Monsieur de Pourceaugnac*" and "*Le Bourgeois Gentilhomme*" (Eng. trans. "The Prodigious Snob") were staged, in 1669 and 1670 respectively, in a makeshift theatre in the south part of the Greek cross on the first floor of the keep. Meanwhile, royal love affairs continued to flourish. In 1684, the King even revealed the new favours that he was ready to grant to Madame de Maintenon while in Chambord. Yet the castle remained first and foremost a political setting in which Louis XIV drew up the decrees against the Calvinists. There was even some discussion of bringing the centre of authority and the Court to Chambord, during the War of Spanish Succession when it seemed that France was about to find itself on the losing side.

The antechamber to the King's apartments, also known as the billiard room, containing the billiard table used by Charles X.

After 1685, the castle remained empty for forty years. Louis XV showed little interest in it but decided to use it as a grace-and-favour residence for his father-in-law, Stanislas Leczinski, King of Poland, who had been exiled from his homeland and who arrived in Chambord in 1725, where he stayed for eight years, until 1733. The locals remembered him as a kindly, benevolent man. He had a number of apartments altered so that they became more comfortable and more convenient to live in. The ceilings were lowered, alcoves and cabinets were built into the rooms to bring them into line with the lifestyle of the day, and the walls were covered with material. The mosquito-infested moat was filled in and gardens were laid out on the lawns. His stay was totally lacking in controversy, but this was not to be the case for his successor.

In 1745, the French Army won a resounding victory at Fontenoy. Their commander-in-chief was Maréchal Maurice de Saxe, to whom Louis XV gave, in grateful recognition of his success and among other honours, the Chambord Estate. In 1748, the Maréchal moved in, living like a monarch and surrounded by a veritable Court. He brought

to the estate days of opulence and luxury, the like of which it had seldom seen before - and would never see again. He gave magnificent parties. He brought Mr. Favart's repertory company to the castle and retained, apparently by slight force, Mrs. Favart for whom he had a theatre designed by the great interior designer, Servandoni. Traces of this theatre can still be seen in the west room on the second floor of the keep. The state room in the king's apartments was altered for him, thanks to a magnificent gift from Louis XV in the form of a red marble fireplace and the woodpanelling from the former Grand Cabinet of the Duchess of Orleans in Versailles. The Maréchal also acquired the services of a regiment of uhlans, the Regiment of Saxony Volunteers, adding to the magnificence and military panache which was part of the Maréchal's everyday life. To provide billets and stabling for the regiment, he ordered the completion of the stables that had been partly built under Hardouin-Mansart on the side of the entrance esplanade.

Maréchal Maurice de Saxe died in strange circumstances in 1750. Officially, it was an improperly-treated

A reception room.

A close-up of the woodpanelling in the King's bedchamber brought to Chambord from Versailles.

chill that killed him; unofficially, he died in a duel with the Prince de Conti. Thereafter, the castle was only occupied from time to time by the Count de Friesen, the Maréchal's nephew. Then, after 1755, it accommodated its governor, Monsieur de Saumery, and the mysterious Count de Saint-Germain. Another governor, the Marquis de Polignac, set up a royal stud in the Maréchal de Saxe's stables in 1781, but he fled from the estate in 1789.

In 1793, the Blois District auctioned off the furniture and left vandals to deal with the carvings, woodwork and mirrors. The castle was put up for sale; nobody wanted it. There was even some talk of having it demolished and the project would almost certainly have succeeded had the architect who had been responsible for its upkeep since 1777, Mr. Marie, not grossly overestimated the cost of demolition. As a result, the inconceivable project was shelved.

It was then that a purpose was sought for Chambord. English Quakers had offered to buy the estate so that one hundred and fifty children could live and work there. Was it to become an Agricultural College or a school for the children of those holding the Legion of Honour? No decision was taken and, instead, it was used as a fodder barn, powder and saltpeter workshop, and the headquarters of the 15th Cohort of the Legion of Honour.

In 1809, Napoléon I raised the Chambord Estate to the rank of Principality of Wagram and gifted it to Maréchal Berthier, on condition that he restored the castle using the pension he received and the income from the estate itself. The Maréchal paid Chambord a lightning visit and died, leaving a widow who was so poor that, after undertaking forest clearance on a massive scale, she decided to sell the entire castle and estate in 1820. It seemed that the "Black Gang" was ready to descend on the castle and use it as a source of building stone.

It was saved thanks to the efforts of Count Adrien de Calonne. He had the idea of launching a nationwide fund to buy it back and, in the name of France, give it to the newborn son of the assassinated Duke de Berry, in 1821. Henri, Duke of Bordeaux, the last of the Bourbon dynasty, took the title of Count of Chambord after 1830. He lived in exile and only came to Chambord for a few days in 1871, but he used all the income from the estate for the upkeep of

A Saxony ceramic stove.
The Maréchal de Saxe had four such stoves
installed to heat his apartments.

A close-up of the manganese decoration
on the ceramic tiles.

A medallion showing the coat-of-arms of Maréchal Berthier.

be able to house part of the collections usually found in the Louvre. In 1945, fire destroyed the south-west tower on the keep but it was rebuilt.

Inside the castle, the 16th, 17th and 18th-century interiors were recreated in the apartments. But it was impossible to control the temperature and humidity levels and there could be no question of displaying valuable furniture, tapestries, paintings, or *objets d'art*. They could only be described and left to the imagination through a few rare examples.

The fragility of the tuft, the marshland underneath the building, and the ethereal daring of the superstructures, added to the almost constant abandonment of the castle in the past, have resulted in a vital need for almost permanent rebuilding work.

A bust of the Count of Chambord.

the park and castle which was, by then, in a highly dilapidated state according to eye witnesses of the day. When he died in 1883, he bequeathed the estate to his nephews, Henri de Bourbon, Count of Bardi, and Robert de Bourbon, Duke of Parma. They commissioned a father-and-son firm of architects named Desbois to carry out major restoration work, including the lantern tower.

Questions continued to be asked as to the possible use of Chambord. In 1871, it was used as a military hospital for the war-wounded and was heated by burning most of the woodpanelling. In 1921, there were suggestions that it should be turned into a car race track some six miles long, backed up by a veritable industrial estate.

In 1914, shortly after the outbreak of the First World War, Chambord was sequestrated because its owner, Prince Elie de Bourbon-Parma, was an Austrian national serving under his country's flag.

Using its right of preemption, the State finally purchased it in 1930. The building was in a critical condition but methodical, continous restoration work began in 1931 and was given greater scope after 1965 when two successive laws were placed on the statute books with a view to instigating a programme of restoration. The entire building required attention - roofs, rafters, the huge chimney stacks, the dormer windows and gables, the window frames and the leaking terraces. During the Second World War, the castle had been restored to a sufficiently high standard to

A palace haunted by fairies and knights of old...
Overleaf : *... brought from the Orient to a land of mist.*

CHAMBORD'S PLACE IN LITERATURE

Few buildings have caused so much questioning and visionary literature as Chambord. It has all the mystery of works of genius, which always have more to show and say than we can actually see or understand.

When Moraes, a Portuguese diplomat at François I's Court, wrote before 1541 that in Chambord, "there are four doors opening onto all four corners of the globe", he assimilated the castle to the Biblical description of Jerusalem the Celestial City, steeped in myth and symbolism. And there is an even more striking view in an anonymous work dating from the 18th century, which speaks of "the reflection of the radiant dark city, wise yet foolish, silent yet haunted, that each of us carries within him". Continuing along the same lines as a result of the strong impression made upon him, he even tells of an amazing phenomenon. "There is something strange in this castle. The staircases are laid out in such a way that, if one wants to climb to a room on a floor above, one has to go downstairs and not up. This is a marvellous and prodigious feat of architecture and is difficult to believe for any who have not seen it". But, as Pierre Gascar wrote, "Everything is possible here. Or, to put it another way, everything is true".

Chambord became an integral part of the literary imagination as soon as it was built. Rabelais refers to it as one of the most famous pieces of architecture of its day when describing Thélème Abbey as "one hundred times more magnificent than Bonivet, Chambord or Chantilly.." in which one can admire "a marvellous spiral staircase designed with such symmetry and capacity than six men-at-arms bearing their lances against their thighs could climb it together, right to the top of the building". In the translation of the Spanish chivalrous romance, "*Amadis de Gaul*", commissioned by François I after he had been so impressed with it in Madrid, there are two engravings depicting the marvellous palace belonging to Apollidon the Enchanter in the Isle Ferme. The layout in the form of a Greek Cross with a central spiral staircase and a tall roof bristling with chimney stacks and dormer windows are an exact replica of Chambord.

In the 19th century, opinions varied, ranging from amazement to disdain. Alfred de Vigny wrote, "one would think that, constrained by some wonderful lamp, an oriental geni had picked the castle up during one of the Thousand and One Nights, and carried it away from a land of sunshine to conceal it amidst the fog, with the love of a fine prince. The palace is hidden away like a treasure trove; but the blue-tinted domes, the elegant minarets rounding out onto wide stretches of wall or thrusting their slender points up to the sky, the long terraces overlooking the woods, the ethereal spires swaying in the wind, and the crescent moons interwoven on every colonnade would all suggest that the palace is in the kingdoms of Baghdad or Kashmir, if the blackened walls covered with a thick carpet of moss and ivy and the pale, melancholy sky did not prove that this was a land of rain. The base of this strange building is, though, full of elegance and mystery. It is a double staircase, with two interwoven spirals rising from the very depths of the building to the topmost heights of the towers, and beyond to the lantern tower or traceried chamber, bearing a gigantic fleur-de-lys that is visible from far away. It is almost impossible to see how the layout was designed. It looks like a brief thought, a brilliant idea that suddenly took form, a dream given reality".

Victor Hugo told his friends, "You cannot imagine how singularly beautiful it is. All the magic, all the poetry, all the folly come together in the admirable strangeness of this fairytale palace taken straight from the pages of a tale of chivalry," it is the "Alhambra Palace of France".

Chateaubriand was equally astonished. "Chambord has only one double staircase so that visitors can go down and up without seeing each other. Everything in the palace is designed to emphasise the mysteries of war and love. The building becomes increasingly perfect at every stage. There are tiny grooves beside the steps, like the stairs in cathedral turrets. Seen from a distance, the building forms an arabesque. It looks like a woman, her hair streaming out in the wind. From close up, the woman fades into the masonry and becomes one with the towers. It is Clorinda leaning on ruins.... a copy of a warring woman at the time of death. If ever Chambord were destroyed, we should never again be able to see the earliest Renaissance style anywhere else, for in Venice it has been combined with later features. The element that gave Chambord its beauty, was its abandonment..."

"The radiant dark city".

A totally different opinion was voiced by Flaubert who visited Chambord in 1847 while travelling on foot. "We walked along the empty galleries and through the abandoned rooms in which spiders spin their webs across François I's salamander emblems. A desolate feeling envelops you at the sight of so much misery; there is nothing beautiful about it. Yet this is no generalised ruin... It is shameful poverty, brushing its threadbare coat in order to appear decent. The parquet flooring is repaired in one room, and left to rot in the next... It is sad, and totally lacking in grandeur. It seems as if everything possible had been done to outrage poor old Chambord... It was given to a whole list of different people, as if nobody wanted it, and wanted to keep it. The castle looks as if it has almost never been used and has always been too big. It is like an abandoned hotel in which travellers have not even left their names on the walls".

Yet another view was expressed by the Socialist journalist and politician, Félix Pyat, writing in the rural encyclopaedia published in the middle of the 19th century. "There are also a few buildings, relics of times past, which prove that the land was controlled before it was poor. Among them is Chambord, with its domes reminiscent of the minarets of the Orient. Chambord, the folly of François I, just as Versailles was the folly of Louis XIV. Chambord, if we may be forgiven this digression, was one of the most superb fantasies of men who sought nothing but the impossible, men who held the elements and their subjects in tyrannical sway, men who enjoyed changing solitude into towns, caverns into Capitols. The general layout of Chambord, set in the depths of a wood, represented the entire social structure of its day. In the middle was royalty or central authority topped by a haughty crown; in the wings were the chapel with its Cross on a slightly lower level and the towers with humbler crenelations, representing the clergy and the nobility both of which were subordinate to the power of the monarch; then came the lower buildings, clambering around the supreme edifice, just as the people clamber around the throne. Chambord stood in the lazy woodlands and stubble of Sologne with all the luxury and strength of its freestone, like a living memorial to the slavery of times past, like an insult to the misery and poverty of today".

The south wall of the keep.

Equally caustic, but in a different way, was the opinion expressed by the American novelist, Henry James, in his "Little Tour in France". He wrote, "Seen from below, the castle would give the impression of being bowed down by the profusion of protuberances on the upper storeys if the enormous circumference of its round towers did not confer upon it an immovable lateral foundation... These towers exaggerate exaggeration itself. I am going to take the risk of being accused of bad taste, and say that even if it was impressive, Chambord seemed to me to have something rather stupid about it. The problem is that it does not represent anything precise. Despite its many ups-and-downs, it has not had a very interesting history." "The great staircase... is an example of a truly majestic sense of humour and, in many ways, sets the tone for Chambord as a whole."

Very recently, Pascal Quignard [16] managed to regain a degree of wonderment. "In the morning,..... he had strolled round the lakes at Chambord. Without believing it to be real, he entered the vast, empty castle - an uncertain castle,

an unfinished castle, a castle that had never been lived in, a castle as white as the shroud that covers the ghosts of the silver screen, as white as a *nougat mandorlato* nibbled on a trip to Florence, as white as a plate of celeriac. This was the whitest and most beautiful ruin in France, and had never been anything else than the building site of a ruin. As he stepped into the main hall, he again smelled the odour of fresh sap, leeks, and damp white plaster that were characteristic of the vast palace lost in the forest amidst the sounder of wild sows with their young and the bevy of stags. The immense rooms had never contained any furniture and it was this that made them look, in some ways, even larger, as if designed for ogres or gods... This castle had never come to life. It was nothing but an immense act of birth, ceaselessly impeded, "a palace of dreams".

CHAMBORD IN CLOSE-UP

The various types of symbolism that some people have tried to see in Chambord, and the impression that the castle always left on observers, have often led to inaccurate descriptions of its main features. An anonymous visitor, who

---

(16) Pascal Quignard, *Les escaliers de Chambord*, pub. Gallimard, 1989, pp. 50-51.

The south wall of the keep.

came to Chambord in the 18th century, even went so far as to say that the staircase was laid out in such a way that, in order to move to a lower storey, one had to go upstairs! It has been said that the castle had up to 440 rooms, but although this figure is still quoted today, it does not take account of the many alterations carried out since the 17th century and should now be revised, downwards. There are those who spoke of "more chimneys than there are days in the year", or who claimed that the castle had 365 windows. But does the symbolism of these figures really reflect reality? No, they should be taken as an rough approximation, as should the figure of 80 staircases and 800 capitals on the pillars. However, it is true that Chambord has kept its secrets with regard to these points.

Decorative features on the facades

The decorative features on the façades comply with a principle that is repeated in an almost identical fashion on each of the buildings. The upper storeys are separated horizontally by a double band of moulding and vertically by flat pilasters which extend upwards from one floor to the next. This forms the grid pattern that was characteristic of the early Renaissance in France. The features of the later Renaissance, i.e. the use of pillars and capitals that are more reminiscent of Ancient Greece and Rome, are only seen here on the buildings completed after 1543, such as the traceried outer staircases in the corners of the François I and Henri II courtyards, and on a few of the dormer windows.

At the top of the keep is a massive carved cornice similar to the one in Blois with its modilions and shells. It provides support for the balustrade on the terrace from which members of the Court used to watch the hunt if they were not taking part themselves.

The non-symetrical facades on the keep

The four walls of the keep are not identical. Although they all have three large windows or French windows in the centre on each storey, they are flanked to right and left either by other windows or by an arched gallery leading to the towers. In fact, only the north and east walls are symmetrical. The north wall overlooks the great flowerbed and has windows across the entire width of the keep while the east wall, overlooking the François I courtyard, has an arched gallery to each side of the central windows. On the west and, more particularly, the south side containing the main entrance, however, there is no attempt at any form of symmetry.

The south-west tower in the keep.

It is easy to understand why if one looks at the design. Each quarter apartment includes one large chamber with two wide windows at the end. However, the layout of the apartments varied from one quarter to another. This resulted in a change in the direction of the windows and a degree of irregularity in the façades. The question remains as to why this layout was chosen.

There are two hypothesis in this respect. One of them states that, quite simply, this was the design drawn by Domenico da Cortona and that the four quarter apartments were built to face outwards like the south-west quarter. On the model for this quarter, the arched galleries leading to the towers were then regrouped in symmetrical fashion on the south and north walls. But, in 1526, François I decided that the royal apartments should be installed in the northeast tower in the outer wall and that the chapel should be in the north-west tower. This meant that the arched galleries linking the chapel and the rooms in the keep had to

The terraces : a capital decorated with carved foliage.

The lantern tower and upper sections of the castle.

wise movement, like the central staircase, so that all four walls would have had the same dissymetrical design, and the castle as a whole would have been steeped in an impression of eddy-like motion. There are three quarters which still show this layout, to the south-east, south-west and north-west. The king's later decision to add wings and towers to the keep which would contain his apartments and the chapel is said to have required a change of direction for the apartment in the north-east quarter so that the external arched gallery could be built along the east wall to provide a link between the keep and the royal apartments.

The terraces

The terrace resembles a veritable village, with streets crossing each other at right angles, like the rooms on the upper floors just below it, a central square around the lantern tower resembling the square around a church, a gallery running round the outside of the entire terrace, and corners and recesses that were, it was said, highly suitable for amorous intrigues. There are also square pavilions with tall

The terraces : a support with figurative carving.

run along the east and west walls of the keep. As a result, the apartments in the corresponding quarters had to be displaced through an angle of 90°. It could be argued that this had nothing to do with the question of symmetry, as long as all the apartments were displaced in the same way. But the apartment in the south-west quarter was already partly built. Because of this, the only way of preserving the symmetry of the east wall opposite the royal apartments was to adopt the layout that we see today, even if it was unsatisfactory.

Another hypothesis [17] refers to an imaginative study of eddies and turbines undertaken by Leonardo da Vinci in his capacity as an engineer. He is said to have designed an unusual layout for the keep at Chambord in which each of the apartments would have faced one of the cardinal points on the compass. This would have created a sense of clock-

(17) This hypothesis has been developed by Jean-Marie Pérouse de Mont-clos, Director of Research in the *Centre National de Recherches*

The terraces : a shell-shaped niche.

roofs, and the pepperpot roofs on the towers, topped by lantern turrets. And the entire layout bristles like a romantic vision of a Gothic mediaeval period with turrets topped by tiny domes, immense chimney stacks covered wtih mouldings, vast dormer windows to provide light for the two storeys in the attic, and the gable decorated with forms and figures that are full of imagination. Over all this, there are pilasters and pillars with ornate capitals, geometrical figures carved in relief, shell-shaped niches, symbols and royal monograms. On the most inaccessible parts of the roof are tiny figures, one of them blowing a hunting horn, another dressed in Court costume, an entire population of *putti* riding swirls of dolphins, leaning nonchalantly against the topmost point of a gable or standing proudly at the very top of a curved pediment, and a large group of salamanders, firepots and fleurs-de-lys. Geometrically-shaped slates add to the general exuberance through colours ranging from blue-black to golden-white, which, thanks to the play of light on the carvings in relief during the day and at night, bring to the stone an infinite variety of colours depending on the season of the year. Sometimes the slate even resembles marble.

The terraces : a capital decorated with carved foliage.

And then, overlooking the terrace and all its features, is the great lantern tower above the central staircase, a tower that has as much tracery as it can take, supported on eight great piers and as ornate as the remainder of the terrace. In fact, there is a tendency to forget that this is a veritable feat of architectural skill, an exceptional work of art in the history of architecture.

The apartments and staircases in the keep

Understanding the layout of the apartments by looking at a plan or, if you can, by taking a stroll through them, is one thing; but it is quite another to pass from one storey to the next, from floor to mezzanine. For this is based on a rigorous system of multiple staircases, all of them spiral, and all of them running through the complex body of the castle. Some of them, like the outside staircases in the

The Henri II staircase.

The François I staircase.

François I and Henri II courtyards or the extraordinary double-spiral central staircase rising to the terrace are monumental, and constitute glorious decorative features. Others, though, and there are many of them, are more discreet or almost totally concealed, so that visitors do not even suspect their existence. These are the tiny narrow spiral staircases leading to the mezzanine in each apartment or the larger spiral steps leading from basement to the very top of the tall roofs, six levels of apartments and rooms.

Originally, the Cross-shaped rooms were designed as passageways, veritable "streets" leading to the apartments that were often filled with craftsmen and traders, and, in greater numbers, guards. They were, in fact, called "guardrooms". Because of this, they were never furnished. But during the great royal festivities held by François I or Louis XIV, tapestries and valuable materials quickly turned them into reception rooms. In the 18th century, when the castle was lived in on a permanent basis, the rooms were furnished and the walls covered with tapestries.

One of the second-floor rooms in the arms of the Cross-shaped layout.

The keep was reserved for the Court. Each quarter apartment on every floor is an independent unit with all the rooms normally in use in those days. The apartments are reached via the Cross-shaped rooms. The main chamber has a high ceiling and opens onto three small rooms with low ceilings topped by another three identical rooms on a mezzanine. The two levels are linked by a small spiral staircase built into the thickness of the wall. They were used as a dressing room, private chapel and bedroom for family or servants. In general, though, there are three other ways of reaching these small rooms on the mezzanine without entering the main chamber. This provided flexibility for domestic functions - or conspiracies.

The apartments in the towers are smaller. Their main chamber is flanked by two other rooms and the mezzanines are reached by a small internal spiral staircase or by the steps rising from the basement to the attics of the castle, outside the apartment itself. This access was highly unsuitable for intrigue.

The rooms open to the public today were subdivided into smaller units at various periods of their history depending on the needs of those living in the castle. This increased the possibilities as regards living space and passageways.

Most of the rooms have a fireplace and all the flues rise to the immense chimney stacks bristling on the roof. The flues from the ground floor have a total height of 137 ft. On the other hand, the latrines, built using a system which ensured that the smell did not rise through the building as a whole, were only accessible from the ground floor or the attics.

The cabinet in François I's apartments with its fireplace and stove.

Overleaf : *The double-spiral staircase.*

The double-spiral staircase

The central, one might say the focal, point of interest is worth much more than a cursory glance. It is a double-spiral staircase, a prodigious piece of building the like of which is unknown anywhere else in the world. It is built within a square measuring 29 ft. x 29 ft. and the start of the two intertwined spirals are diametrically opposed yet each of the staircases leads up to the same point on the two upper floors and the terrace. The staircase is traceried and has no well. Instead, it is supported on eight pillars between which the handrails of the bannisters unroll and unwind. The core is hollow so that light floods in from the lantern tower above. The base of the staircase forms a passageway and, as you climb, there are openings that enable you to see those climbing or descending the other staircase without ever finding yourself face to face with them.

The decorative features on the staircase are quite outstanding and you must take time to stop and look at the infinite profusion of carvings. All the pilasters inside and out are topped by capitals with superb carvings. The subtlety of the work reflects a lively imagination that has created ever-differing forms containing a whole world of plants and animals, vast numbers of facetious human figures carved with a delectable facility. This is one of the major masterpieces of French Renaissance decorative carving.

Yet this magnificent piece of architecture is much more than a staircase in a symbolic position. It is a veritable theatrical backcloth reflecting the image that royal power had of itself. It is like a game for those who climb it and who, as they catch sight of others on the staircase, attempt to join them without ever succeeding. It gave those in the rooms a constant spectacle of people going up and down.

In her "Memoirs", Mademoiselle de Montpensier, the Grande Mademoiselle, daughter of Gaston of Orleans, recounts dazzling tales of childhood games with her father in the staircase "built in such a way that one person can go up and the other down without ever meeting, even though they can see each other". In more recent times, the novelist Pascal Quignard situates the games of other children in this "gigantic, great, white, central staircase rising in the centre of the keep" : "they shouted with delight as they climbed" the two flights of steps in Chambord "which superimposed their revolution so that they could see the others all the time without ever meeting them". [18]

(18) Pascal Quignard, id. pp. 50-51.

The chapel

Although invisible from the outside except for the Cross on its roof, the chapel is rather strangely contained in the tower and west wing. It fills the first and second floors and is more spacious than is usual in castle chapels. It is decorated like the remainder of Chambord, and is rather more reminiscent of the styles of Ancient Greece and Rome, with its twin columns, false windows with pediments, and the entire gamut of architectural decoration that was to form the basis of Classicism and that the Italian architect, Serlio, had just introduced into France. This made it the most modern building of its day. Each stage of the building bears the hallmark of its designer. There is François I's salamander, Henri II's monogram which was removed in the 19th century, and the 'L' and sun emblem of Louis XIV.

The chapel.

CONCLUSION

However hard one tries, one can never totally understand Chambord. One is always left with a fabulous but abstract concept which is both rational and ephemeral, rather than with a castle designed for a clear purpose, such as war, brilliant pleasure, or as a quiet place to live. Chambord is impossible to live in, has never been lived in, and is the finest example of this enigma.

There is an almost total lack of any connection between the unique wealth of decorative features or the ideas behind them and the forest in which the castle was built, with no transition other than a simple clearing. It is utopian, in the sense given to the term by its inventor, Sir Thomas More, in 1516 [19] when Chambord was still in the design stage. It does not date from any specific time nor does it fit any particular place. It is a stranger to its own environment, "neither Gothic nor modern", as Félibien said.

If any other argument were needed, suffice it to say that the only way of really appreciating its coherent architecture is by observing it from a plane. Yet nobody could do this when it was built, except perhaps, in their mind's eye, François I and Leonardo da Vinci, who dreamed of it before having it built?

(19) Sir Thomas More was an English Humanist and statesman, and the author of a political and social novel entitled "Utopia", a neologism based on the Greek "ou" and "topos" meaning "nowhere".

Overleaf : *A general view of the castle from the great "Courtyard".*

Sunrise behind Chambord Castle.

ROOMS OPEN TO THE PUBLIC

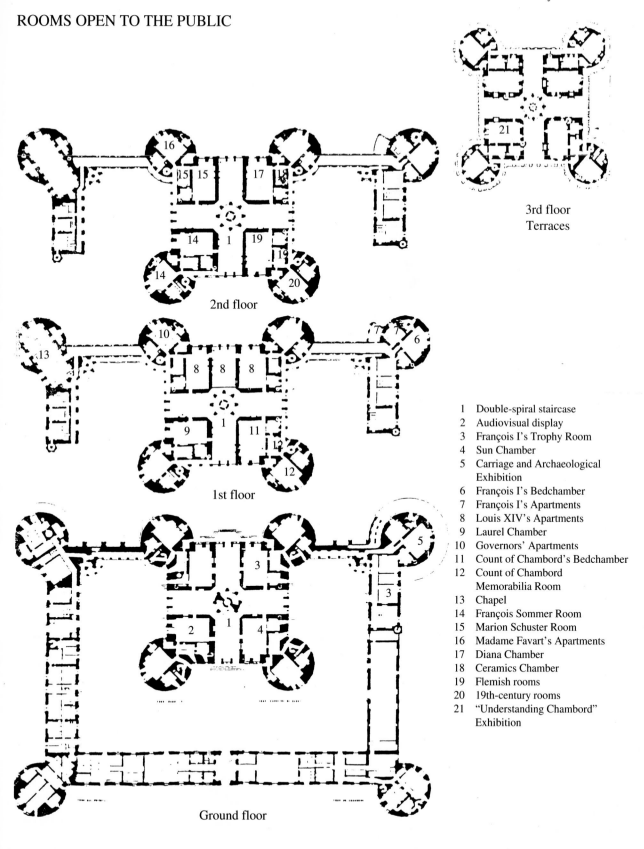

3rd floor
Terraces

2nd floor

1st floor

Ground floor

1 Double-spiral staircase
2 Audiovisual display
3 François I's Trophy Room
4 Sun Chamber
5 Carriage and Archaeological Exhibition
6 François I's Bedchamber
7 François I's Apartments
8 Louis XIV's Apartments
9 Laurel Chamber
10 Governors' Apartments
11 Count of Chambord's Bedchamber
12 Count of Chambord Memorabilia Room
13 Chapel
14 François Sommer Room
15 Marion Schuster Room
16 Madame Favart's Apartments
17 Diana Chamber
18 Ceramics Chamber
19 Flemish rooms
20 19th-century rooms
21 "Understanding Chambord" Exhibition

TABLE OF CONTENTS

REFERENCES

Babelon (Jean), *Châteaux de France au siècle de la Renaissance*, Flammarion/Picard, 1989
Guillaume (Jean), *Comprendre Chambord*, CNMHS, 1983
Jacquart (Jean), *François I*, Fayard, 1988
Lagoutte (Claudine), *Chambord*, Ouest-France/CNMHS, 1983
Lecoq (Anne-Marie), *François I imaginaire*, Macula, 1987
Architectures en Région Centre, coll. Le Guide du Patrimoine, Hachette/Conseil Régional, 1987.

PRACTICAL INFORMATION

Whether you pay Chambord a brief visit or stay just a little bit longer, you will find an Information Centre, hotel, restaurants, souvenir shops and a Loir-et-Cher wine kiosk. You may like to take a closer look at the forest and its wildlife - the stags, wild boar and other animals that roam free. There are 700 hectares of forest open to the public, to visit on foot, horseback or in a carriage. The forest has waymarked footpaths (including the long-distance GR3 and service paths), game observatories, and fully-equipped picnic areas. You can visit the castle on your own or, depending on the season, take a guided tour. Environmental study and architecture workshops are available on request and guided tours can be arranged for parties of schoolchildren or adults. For all further information, contact the *Commissariat à l'Aménagement du Domaine*, 41250 Chambord. Tel. 54 20 31 50, fax 54 20 34 69

PHOTOGRAPHIC CREDITS

Anquetin : 39 t.
Boulé : 2 t.
Bricker : 21, 32, 34, 37, 38, 39 b, 40, 41, 42, 43, 44, 50, 51, 52, 53, 54, 55, 56, 57, 58, 59, 60.
Forget : 3, 4, 5, 8, 9, 10, 11, 2, 13, 15, 18 t, 23, 28, 29, 36, 45, 46, 47, 48, 61.
Trézin : 2 m, 6-7, 16-17, 18 b, 20, 22, 26, 30, 31, 33, 35, 49.

Cet ouvrage a été imprimé par l'imprimerie Aubin à Ligugé (86)
I.SB.N. 2.7373.1149.7 - N° d'éditeur : 2478.01.06.06.92
Dépôt légal : juin 1992